GETTING TO KNOW
THE U.S. PRESIDENTS

B E N J A M I N
HARRISON

TWENTY-THIRD PRESIDENT
1889 – 1893

WRITTEN AND ILLUSTRATED BY MIKE VENEZIA

CHILDREN'S PRESS®
A DIVISION OF SCHOLASTIC INC.
NEW YORK   TORONTO   LONDON   AUCKLAND   SYDNEY
MEXICO CITY   NEW DELHI   HONG KONG
DANBURY, CONNECTICUT

Reading Consultant: Nanci R. Vargus, Ed.D., Assistant Professor, School of Education, University of Indianapolis

Historical Consultant: Marc J. Selverstone, Ph.D., Assistant Professor, Miller Center of Public Affairs, University of Virginia

Photographs © 2006: Art Resource, NY/National Portrait Gallery, Smithsonian Institution, Washington DC, USA: 16 (George Peter Alexander Healy), 3 (T.C. Steele); Bridgeman Art Library International Ltd., London/New York/Theodor Groll/Private Collection: 11; Corbis Images: 13 (Bettmann), 31 (David J. & Janice L. Frent Collection), 32 (Parker); Library of Congress: 17 (Currier & Ives), 18, 19, 30; PictureHistory.com: 10 left; President Benjamin Harrison Home: 10 right; Steve Wolowina: 26; Superstock, Inc./Eyre Crowe: 12; The Art Archive/Picture Desk/Culver Pictures: 29.

Colorist for illustrations: Dave Ludwig

Library of Congress Cataloging-in-Publication Data

Venezia, Mike.
  Benjamin Harrison / written and illustrated by Mike Venezia.
     p. cm. — (Getting to know the U.S. presidents)
  ISBN 0-516-22628-2 (lib. bdg.)   0-516-25400-6 (pbk.)
  1. Harrison, Benjamin, 1833-1901—Juvenile literature. 2. Presidents—United States—Biography—Juvenile literature. I. Title.
  E702.V46 2006
  973.8'6'092—dc22

                              2005012094

A portrait of Benjamin Harrison by T.C. Steele (National Portrait Gallery, Smithsonian Institution)

Benjamin Harrison was the twenty-third president of the United States. He was born in 1833 in North Bend, Ohio. Benjamin was born into a family that was very active in serving its country. Ben's great-grandfather was a signer of the Declaration of Independence. His grandfather, William Henry Harrison, was the ninth president of the United States. Ben's father served as a U.S. congressman.

Benjamin Harrison was an excellent public speaker. Whenever he ran for public office, he held the attention of thousands of people. Crowds loved his sense of humor and were inspired by his ideas.

In small groups, however, Ben was
strangely shy and not very friendly. He was
so stiff at times that he became known as
the Human Iceberg.

Benjamin Harrison grew up on his family's 600-acre farm. He had three brothers and four sisters. There were lots of wilderness areas in Ohio in the early 1800s. Ben loved to spend time swimming and fishing in the rivers and streams near his home. His favorite activity, though, was hunting squirrels, rabbits, and ducks.

Ben Harrison's father believed in the importance of education. There weren't many schools in the area, so Ben's father built a one-room schoolhouse right near his farm. He hired teachers, too. Ben's parents were determined to give their children the best education possible.

Benjamin loved reading and was an excellent student. When he was a little older, he attended an academy called Farmer's College. Then he went to Miami University in Oxford, Ohio.

Students at Miami University were expected to be in their rooms by 7:00 PM every night. One time, Ben sneaked out at night to go to a dance at a girl's school that was just across the street. It was during this time that he met Caroline Scott, whose nickname was Carrie. By the time Ben graduated, he and Carrie had fallen in love and had decided to get married.

Benjamin Harrison and Caroline Harrison during the mid-1800s

While Ben was at Miami University, he made up his mind to become a lawyer. He studied law and worked at a lawyer's office in the nearby city of Cincinnati, Ohio.

Ben passed his law exam in 1854. He didn't like Cincinnati, though. He thought it was too crowded and dirty. Ben and Carrie decided to move to Indianapolis, Indiana. They set up a home and Ben started a law business there.

Indianapolis was a growing city, but it still had lots of farm country and wilderness surrounding it. As Ben's law business began to grow, he and Carrie started their family. They had a son, Russell, and a daughter, Mary Scott.

This painting shows how Indianapolis looked when Benjamin Harrison lived and worked there in the mid-1800s.

A painting from the 1850s showing people being sold at a slave market in the South

While Ben was building a successful career as a lawyer, he became interested in politics. At the time, a big argument was brewing in the United States between the northern and southern states. Southerners believed slavery should be legal. As time went on, more and more northerners thought slavery should be abolished, or stopped.

Because Ben was from the northern state of Indiana, and was definitely against slavery, he decided to join a new political organization called the Republican Party. Members of the new party believed that slavery should not be allowed to spread beyond the South into new territories or states.

Many people in Indiana, including Benjamin Harrison, thought slavery was wrong. This illustration shows slaves arriving at an Indiana farm that was a major stop on the Underground Railroad.

Ben became very busy campaigning for Republican candidates running for office. One of the candidates he helped was Abraham Lincoln. Ben even ran for an election himself. In 1860, Benjamin Harrison was elected Supreme Court Reporter of the State of Indiana.

It was a great job for someone interested in politics. Ben's responsibility was to keep accurate records of all the cases that came before the court.

Ben was allowed to publish the reports and keep whatever profits he made from selling them. More importantly, the job allowed Ben to meet politicians and learn how they worked with each other.

A portrait of President Abraham Lincoln by George Peter Alexander Healy (National Portrait Gallery, Smithsonian Institution)

At the same time Benjamin Harrison began his job as court reporter, Abraham Lincoln began his job as the sixteenth president of the United States. Tensions between the North and South had grown so bitter by then that the southern states decided to secede, or leave, the United States. They formed their own country, the Confederate States of America.

Soon the Civil War began. President Lincoln called for volunteers to fight in the war. At first, Ben held back. He had a family and relatives to support and a business to run. Two years later, however, when the North needed more men, Ben volunteered.

This illustration shows U.S. troops defending Fort Sumter after Confederate forces attacked the fort on April 12, 1861. This attack began the Civil War.

Benjamin Harrison started as a lieutenant. He was asked to recruit men to form an army group, or regiment. Ben was later promoted to the rank of colonel and became a brave leader. Although he never liked fighting in battles, Ben guided his men to victory time after time.

Colonel Benjamin Harrison on horseback

Colonel Harrison fought bravely in many Civil War battles, including the 1864 Battle of Resaca (above).

Colonel Harrison's men called him "Little Ben" because he was on the small side. Ben was greatly honored because he knew the men gave him the nickname as a sign or respect. At the end of the war, "Little Ben" Harrison was promoted to brigadier general.

Catchy nicknames were important in politics. People were more likely to remember a candidate who had a one-of-a-kind name. Ben's grandfather, William Henry Harrison, had a great nickname. He was called Old Tippecanoe after a famous battle he had fought in.

Unfortunately, when Ben Harrison ran for governor of Indiana in 1876, he was given a nickname that wasn't very helpful at all. Ben's opponent, James "Blue Jeans" Williams, started calling Ben "Kid Gloves" Harrison. Kid gloves are soft, expensive goatskin gloves that rich people wore at the time.

Ben lost the election for governor. He didn't lose because of his nickname, but it didn't help that some people believed Ben was a stuck-up rich guy.

Ben didn't mind too much that he lost the election. He had plenty of things to do. He continued running a successful law business and helped other Republican candidates get elected.

In 1880, Benjamin Harrison himself was elected a U.S. senator. Then, in 1888, he was nominated by the Republican Party to run for president of the United States.

Ben ran against President Grover Cleveland. The campaign of 1888 was one of the politest in American history. No one made up harmful stories about the other person's past life. No one was called a crook or liar, either. Both men treated each other with respect. This behavior was much different from almost every presidential campaign before or after.

The election of 1888 was very close, but Benjamin Harrison won. When Ben moved into the White House, he brought his entire family with him, including relatives, grandchildren, and Old Whiskers, the family goat. Even though the White House had been redecorated a few years earlier, the Harrisons found it had been badly neglected in other ways.

It had leaky pipes, mildew and mold on the walls, and rotted wooden stairways. Mrs. Harrison was able to get some money from Congress to spiff the place up. She had bugs and mice removed, added new plumbing and electricity, and had the whole place scrubbed and painted.

President Harrison supported laws to preserve the nation's great forestlands.

President Harrison did much more than fix up the White House. Even though some history experts think Benjamin Harrison was just a so-so president, he actually dealt with lots of important matters and faced serious issues.

For example, President Harrison was one of the nation's first conservationists. He signed laws that preserved millions of acres of forestland in the western states of Wyoming and California. He also was very concerned about people's civil rights. He wanted African Americans in the South to be treated fairly and worked hard to protect their right to vote.

President Harrison was very successful in working out agreements for trading products and goods with foreign countries. His ideas worked well and were used for years by future presidents.

President Harrison also supported an important law called the Sherman Anti-Trust Act. Trusts are groups of large, powerful companies. Sometimes these companies would get together to control prices. A super-large company called a monopoly could also control prices by grabbing up smaller companies and becoming the only seller of a product or service.

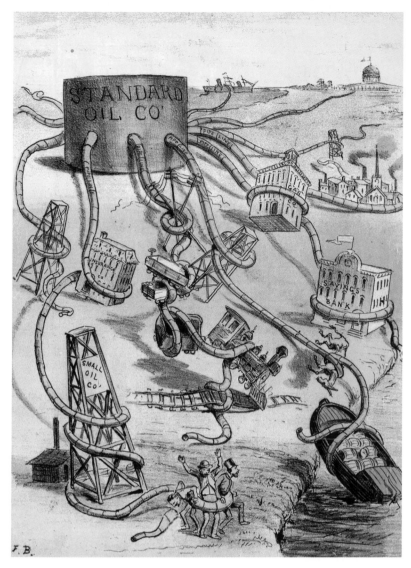

This political cartoon from 1884 shows Standard Oil Company, a huge monopoly, acting like an octopus and "grabbing up" smaller oil companies. President Harrison worked to end monopolies and trusts.

Smaller businesses couldn't compete with trusts and monopolies. These giant businesses could raise prices for their products or services as high as they wanted. The Sherman Anti-Trust Act of 1890 made trusts and monopolies against the law. It was an important first step toward controlling unfair business.

PUCK.

THE OPENING OF THE CONGRESSIONAL SESSION.

A political cartoon from the late 1880s showing Congress having to deal with a "monster" surplus

When President Harrison started his new job, the U.S. government had an unusual problem. It had too much money! The president and Congress had to figure out how to spend it. President Harrison was very generous in giving pensions, or money, to Civil War veterans and their families.

Even though Ben Harrison meant well, many people felt he was giving away too much money. People who weren't getting any government help became angry.

President Harrison also supported a high tax on products that came into the United States from foreign countries. This kind of tax is called a tariff. The tariff was meant to get people to buy American products. However, American manufacturers responded by raising their prices. By the time the next election came along, President Harrison had lost a lot of support.

Benjamin Harrison during his later years, with his grown daughter and grandson

President Harrison didn't get reelected in 1892. The loss was partly Harrison's own fault. His shyness turned people off, and he often refused to listen to advice from his friends and supporters.

Ben was also distracted and upset during the election. His wife, Carrie, had been very ill. Sadly, she died two weeks before election day.

Ben Harrison seemed almost relieved that he lost the election, and gladly went back home to Indiana. He returned to his law practice, even arguing cases before the Supreme Court.

A few years later, Ben Harrison remarried. He kept busy raising a new baby daughter and giving lectures around the country. Benjamin Harrison died in Indianapolis on March 13, 1901.